William Wilberforce

Britain's Great Emancipator

BY JOHN HOLZMANN

 Avyx

Cover illustration by Ken Tunell.
Cover design by Daniel Westby.
Avyx Inc.
8022 S. Grant Way
Littleton, CO 80122-2705
USA
Email: main@avyx.com
Printed in the United States of America.

TABLE OF CONTENTS

AUTHOR'S NOTE

This book is meant to introduce fourth grade students to a man who made a profound difference in British—and, actually, world—history.

Out of consideration for the primary audience, I have simplified the wordings of virtually all quotes in this book—even the words of other biographers. It has been my intent to preserve the meanings, even if the words are different.

For books that preserve the integrity of high scholarship, including precise quotations, ellipses, source references, and so forth, please refer to the books listed in the bibliography at the back of this current volume!

Thank you.

It is my hope that readers will gain new insight into what well-disposed and disciplined people can accomplish when they conduct themselves with integrity, kindness and dedication . . . and, as Wilberforce did, stand steadfastly upon principle.

John Holzmann
25 January 2014

CHAPTER 1: THE GOOD LIFE

You would have never expected Billy Wilberforce to make any difference in the world.

He came from a wealthy family. And wealth can make it easier for someone to do great things. But the people Billy Wilberforce knew rarely used their wealth to do great things. They used their money to have fun!

When Billy was an old man, he said his mother had chosen friends for him only to help him feel happy. She didn't choose friends that might encourage him to think deep thoughts or who would cause him to think about matters of importance. She wanted him to live as carefree as possible.

Even when he was in college, he said, it seemed as if his professors mostly wanted to keep him from working hard or doing anything useful. "If, occasionally, I looked like I was studying," he said, "some of my professors actually said to me, 'Why should such a wealthy man like you trouble himself with study?' " In other words, "A wealthy man like you ought *not* to study."

If Billy's friends, his teachers, and even his mother seemed interested in keeping him from doing anything useful, Billy's body, too, made such ambitions hard to imagine.

For one thing, Billy was considered unattractive.

He had a huge nose.

He was short.

His spine was so terribly curved that he looked hunched over and twisted.

And to top it all off, he was often sick. Really sick. Several times in his life he almost died from problems with his digestive system.

When Billy grew up, people knew him not as Billy, but by his given name, William, or, more commonly, by his last name only: Wilberforce. And when that name became famous, people knew he had made a big difference in the world. A very big difference.

* * *

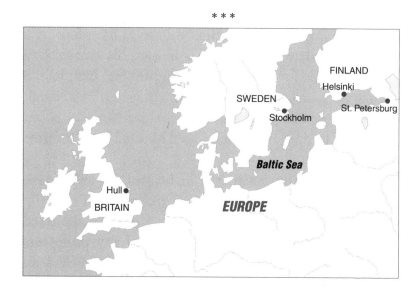

William Wilberforce was born in Hull, England, a shipping city, in 1759. Billy's father had made a fortune by shipping goods to and from the Baltic Sea. The family was rich enough that Billy had everything he could possibly want. A dozen or more servants in the house attended to his every need. They washed his clothes. They made his bed. They helped him dress properly in the morning when he got up, and they helped him to bed when he was ready to sleep at night. And with all of that help, there was very little, indeed, that Billy needed to think about.

By the time he was nine, however, things had changed in the Wilberforce household. Billy's father had died, and his mother sent Billy away to the home of his Aunt Hannah and Uncle William Thornton. Billy came to love his aunt and uncle, and they loved him back. The three of them made a very happy family. Except for one thing.

People thought of Aunt Hannah as a "religious enthusiast"—a religious nut. She followed the teachings of John and Charles Wesley.[1] People like her tried very hard to live their lives according to what they believed the Bible told them to do. For Billy's mother, such a way of life made no sense at all. To begin with, it made no sense to her for a person deliberately to *avoid* pleasure. But to avoid pleasure so that one can go to church and think about sin and salvation and how to live a thoughtful religious life: the idea offended her deeply.

So, when Mrs. Wilberforce received several letters from Billy that indicated he was becoming interested in his aunt's religion, she took the fastest coach she could find to take her to London. She wanted to rescue her son from what she believed was a real evil.

Mrs. Wilberforce wanted her son to have "good" friends, the kind of friends who would help him live a life appropriate to a boy of his social standing, a life of fun and frolic. And so, when she got him back to Hull, Mrs. Wilberforce made sure that young Billy received invitations to all the best parties. And she made sure he spent as many hours as possible with friends who would help him enjoy himself—whether or not he did anything

---

1. *John Wesley* was an Anglican minister who was eventually thrown out of the church for paying too much attention to the poor and downtrodden. He preached in hayfields, mine yards and town squares—places where poor people actually lived and worked. His behavior offended other pastors who thought it was inappropriate to preach outside of a true church building.

John and his brother Charles (who wrote over 6,000 Christian songs including many famous ones like "Hark! The Herald Angels Sing") became the founders of what we know today as the Methodist churches.

useful or meaningful.

Wilberforce commented, later in life, "At that time, Hull was one of the merriest, most pleasant places you could find outside of London. All the leading merchants and their families took great pleasure in attending the theater, balls, and large supper and card parties."

So Wilberforce spent his teen years doing what all the young men of his position in society seemed to do. He attended three, four, and sometimes even five parties a week. The parties included lavish, multi-course dinners, all the fine wine you could drink, and dancing till 2 or 3 in the morning (or even until dawn). Wilberforce spent hours with his friends gambling, drinking, foining[2] and singing. These were the things young men of his position in society were expected to do. And Wilberforce enjoyed these activities all the way through college and beyond.

Wilberforce was smart and had a special way with words so that his friends often congratulated him for his ability to foin. His teachers also recognized his verbal abilities. They would often make him stand up in front of the class to provide his classmates an example of fine diction and elocution. However, partially because he was able to speak and sing so beautifully; partially because his mind was quick; and, partially, as we have seen, because his teachers encouraged him to take life easy, Wilberforce mostly faked his way through school. He never learned the disciplines of study or of careful preparation. Later in life, he confessed that he regretted he had been so lazy during his youth. He believed he could have done

---

2. **Foin:** from a word used in fencing or sword-fighting that means to thrust at an opponent. Here, it means to engage in a verbal contest. You would tell a joke or make a witty comment, and your friends would respond with a joke or comment of their own. Each joke or comment was supposed to be better, sharper, and wittier than the last. Eventually, someone would top them all, and his friends then would congratulate him on how smart he was.

more—if only he had been more focused on studies and other such disciplines while he had been a young man.

Questions[3]

1. When and where was Wilberforce born?

2. What significant event happened when Wilberforce was nine years old?

3. What did Wilberforce's mother not like about Aunt Hannah and Uncle William Thornton?

4. The author claims that Wilberforce had very little in his favor to make him a world-changer. Why is that?

5. What did it mean to "foin"?

6. What kinds of things did Wilberforce and his friends like to do?

7. This chapter begins with a story about how Wilberforce's mother, friends, and even professors at college all encouraged him to play rather than to work hard. In fact, some of his professors actually criticized him for studying: "Why should such a wealthy man like you trouble himself with study?" What do you think? Is there a reason someone—whether wealthy or poor—should study?

---

3. Answers may be found beginning on p. 72.

CHAPTER 2: POLITICS

After he graduated from Cambridge University, William Wilberforce made it his habit to spend almost every evening watching and listening to the debates in the House of Commons. He was fascinated by the verbal give and take. He was also interested in the important matters that the Members of Parliament (MPs) debated.

The British North American colonies (what we now know as the United States) were just then fighting for their independence. Wilberforce wanted to know why his country was at war with the colonies. Why were the colonies fighting? And how did Parliament make its decisions about the colonies?

As he spent time in the gallery night after night,[1] Wilberforce became aware that another young man, William Pitt, was also spending every evening in the gallery. The two soon introduced themselves.

William Pitt was the son of a former Prime Minister. He was only a couple of months older than Wilberforce. He, too, had studied at Cambridge, but in another college. Both men wanted to go into politics—Pitt, because he was passionate about politics; Wilberforce, simply because he couldn't think of anything better to do.

Only a few months after they first met in 1780, Pitt and Wilberforce realized they might be able to fulfill their dreams. An election was to be held that fall, barely a week after Wilberforce turned 21. A man had to be 21 years old to be elected to Parliament. Why not run?

Wilberforce used every means at his disposal to

---

1. The House of Commons at that time began its sessions in the afternoon and normally debated through the evening, sometimes late into the night, and sometimes even till dawn the next morning.

win a seat in Parliament. He used his powerful voice (some called it "the voice of an angel") to make speeches everywhere he could. He used his birthday as an excuse to throw a lavish feast to which he invited all the electors. When the election finally came and the votes were all counted, Wilberforce had won a seat by a landslide. He had received exactly the same number of votes (1,126) as his two opponents had received together.

For Pitt, however, it was another story. He was the one who really cared whether he won or lost, but he failed to get the votes he needed. The two men, obviously, would soon have to part company.

Three months later, however, a wealthy man gave Pitt the right to represent the borough of Appleby, and so Pitt was able to join Wilberforce in the House of Commons.[2]

When Pitt joined Parliament in January, 1781, he and Wilberforce took up their relationship where they had left off. Their friendship blossomed, and they were soon inseparable: not only at Parliament, but "out on the town," too. They ate, drank, foined, played cards, sang and danced. Many nights they simply went to Wilberforce's house where they ate dinner together. They also played practical jokes on one another and on others.

During their first three years in Parliament, Wilberforce became known for his quick wit and charm, but he wielded no power as a politician. Pitt, on the other hand, distinguished himself so much as a politician that, at the age of 24, the King appointed him to be Prime Minister,

---

2. The British Parliament is divided into two "Houses." The **Commons**, or "Lower" House, is composed of popularly elected representatives. The **Lords**, or "Upper" House, was, at that time, composed of noblemen who inherited their seats, and bishops of the Church of England. At the time Pitt and Wilberforce ran for office, there were a few wealthy and influential men who somehow "owned" seats in the Commons which they could then "give" to whomever they wished. It was through such a "gift" that Pitt came to join the Commons.

the most powerful government position besides that of the King himself.[3] No man before or since has ever been raised to Prime Minister at such a young age.

Questions

1. What university did Wilberforce attend?

2. What is an MP?

3. When did the British Parliament tend to do most of its business?

4. What are the names of the two Houses of the British Parliament? Who served in them in Wilberforce's day?

5. What did Pitt do that no man has done before or since?

6. What is the Prime Minister?

---

3. *Prime Minister*, in the British government, is somewhat similar to the U.S. President, Senate Majority Leader, and Speaker of the House all rolled into one. It is an extremely powerful position. The Prime Minister can almost completely control what Parliament will discuss.

CHAPTER 3: A DIVIDED COUNTRY

Wilberforce and his friends enjoyed a manner of life that was far removed from the great majority of people in England at the time.

Members of the upper class, as we have seen, squandered their time and money in singing and dancing, attending large banquets, drinking, foining and gambling. Their waking hours often extended from mid-day till dawn … or from mid-morning until 1 or 2 o'clock in the morning. Their excesses were sometimes the source of legends. One young man lost £10,000—the equivalent of a thousand people's wages for a year!—in a single night's gambling. Others gambled away fortunes of more than a million pounds (though to lose that much usually took a few years).

Men drank to excess. Some writers commented that a couple of Prime Ministers stumbled into Parliament so drunk that they couldn't remain standing on their own power. Such behavior led many people to gossip and snicker, but no one ever reprimanded the Prime Minister for acting that way.

It was the same when young men of the upper classes got together and ran wild through the town at night. At least once, a band of young men knocked down and beat up some elderly watchmen who were standing guard at their posts.

But no one dared say a word.

For the upper classes, it seemed, life was a dream. And they could do no wrong. For people in the lower classes, meanwhile, life was a nightmare. And they could do no right.

While the rich seemed to throw their money away,

many poor people literally worked themselves to death simply trying to earn enough money to put food on the table. It was not uncommon for husbands, wives *and* their children—entire families—to work 13, 14, and sometimes even 16 hours a day six or seven days a week. When they returned home after a day's labor, these people had little energy to do anything besides sleep.

Life was so hard for the lower classes that few people lived beyond their mid-30s.

One could find lower-class women working in the coal mines. They had to carry baskets of coal that weighed 170 pounds or more up and down steep ladders. They carried the baskets hanging them from leather straps wrapped around their foreheads. As you can imagine, such work often led to major injuries and even death.

Besides women, you would also find children in the mines: hundreds of them. One mine had 173 children younger than 8 on its payroll! These children worked a minimum of 12 hours a day—from 6:30 in the morning to 6:30 at night—with no more than half an hour off for lunch (supposing they had any lunch to eat; often they didn't). These children worked a minimum of six days a week.

Needless to say, such children had no hope of learning how to read or of bettering themselves in some way. They could look forward to nothing besides work in the mines for the rest of their lives.

Then there were the chimney sweeps: young boys (some as young as five or six years old) who were hired to crawl up chimneys and clean out the soot that had accumulated there. The job had to be done. If the soot became too thick, it could cause a dangerous fire inside the chimney itself.

Chimney sweeps lived unbelievably dangerous lives. Besides the health hazards they suffered simply from breathing the soot, many died right inside the chimneys they were trying to clean. Boys died of suffocation when they became trapped in a flue, or when thoughtless people lit fires in the fireplaces below while the boys were working in the chimneys. Others died of burns they suffered from fires in the chimneys themselves.

Conditions were just as bad in other trades.

Sailing was a respectable occupation for young men. But from the perspective of the merchant ship owners and their captains, sailors were worthless beasts, men without souls. Sailors were often whipped with the Cat 0' Nine-Tails, a leather whip with nine thongs on the end designed to cut the skin of the victim and cause horrible pain. Many such whippings resulted in permanent injury or death.

* * *

As we have seen, it seemed the rich could do almost any evil and avoid punishment. The poor, meanwhile, seemed unable to escape punishment for even the smallest infraction. Not only were they punished, but the punishments they received were severe.

When Wilberforce was in the Commons, hanging was the prescribed punishment for over 200 crimes. One minor example: if you and your family were starving to death and you found a rabbit living in woods owned by a rich man, you could be hanged if you killed that rabbit for food.

In the middle of this society, divided as it was between rich and poor, there was a third class of people in the British Empire. They were residents against their will.

They were actually poorer than the poor, they suffered greater indignities, and they lacked all freedom.

By the time Wilberforce became a man, they were rarely seen in England itself. Most of them lived in the colonies—especially in the West Indies, the islands of the Caribbean. This third group of people was the slaves. They were men and women who had been captured in Africa, then transported across the Atlantic and sold into slavery.

After being captured, these Black African slaves were placed aboard ships where they were sometimes forced to lie down, chained together side by side, with less than three feet of room between one deck and the next.[1] And they had only inches more than a full body width in which to lie. They were required to remain lying down for the better part of six weeks while the boat crossed the ocean. If the weather was bad, they were forced to lie where they were throughout the storm with no respite. If the storm lasted a week, then they would lie there for a week. They were not permitted to go to a bathroom. If someone got sick and vomited, they and their neighbors had to lie in the vomit. If someone died (as many did), the body stayed where it was until the storm passed.

If the weather was nice, the ship's crew would sometimes bring the slaves on deck to "enjoy" the fresh air. Except, while they were on deck, one of the crew members would crack a whip to keep the slaves "dancing." It was a ghastly form of exercise.

By the time the ship arrived at its destination,

---

1. i.e., the decks where these prospective slaves were forced to lie down were more like shelves or racks in an oven. The slavers—the men who owned and operated the ships—weren't concerned about anyone's comfort. They wanted only to get as many people on board their ships as possible. After all, the more slaves on board, the more profits. And profits seemed to be all they cared about.

sometimes as many as a third of the potential slaves had died. And a large part of the surviving slaves were sick. Those who were sick would be fed and permitted a brief time to recover from the trip across the Atlantic. That was not an act of mercy on the part of their captors. It was so that these slaves would appear healthy and could obtain a good price when they were sold at auction.

There were few if any legal protections given slaves against cruel or inhumane treatment by slave ship captains or masters.

Questions

1. Describe what life was like for wealthy people in Britain at the time Wilberforce first entered Parliament.

2. What was life like for poor people?

3. How about for slaves?

CHAPTER 4: A NEW LIFE

Wilberforce planned to accompany his mother, sister and two female cousins on a trip to the French Riviera in the late fall of 1784. The women were going to spend the winter there.

Before he left on the trip, Wilberforce bumped into one of his favorite teachers from Grammar School.[1] Isaac Milner was a brilliant mathematician and scientist and Wilberforce invited Milner to join him on the trip. He thought Milner would be a better conversation partner than the women would.

And so, that October the two men rode in a separate carriage as they accompanied the women on their journey across Europe.

While in France, Wilberforce absent-mindedly picked up a copy of a book one of his cousins had brought with her. The book was called *The Rise and Progress of Religion*.

Milner saw it and commented. "That's one of the best books ever written."

"You've got to be kidding!" Wilberforce replied in disbelief. "A book on *religion* is 'one of the best ever written'!!?"

"Seriously," Milner replied. "As a matter of fact, I wouldn't mind reading it again on our way back to London."

Wilberforce was astonished that Milner would say such a thing. But considering his admiration for Milner, he decided he would read it and, at Milner's urging, he agreed to discuss it as they rode along.

By the time the men returned to London, the book had obviously made an impact on Wilberforce. He didn't

---

1. The equivalent of elementary school.

behave any differently. His diary included the same kinds of notes it had always included: "Sat up all night," "Danced till five in the morning," and so forth.

But side by side with these notes, he began to make comments that were very different from any he had made before: "_____'s christening: laughter all around; very indecent"; "Shocking dance at the opera, yet the audience unmoved"; "Strange that the most generous men and religious do not see their duties increase with their fortune."

Wilberforce had started to evaluate his own life and the lives and behaviors of others. For the first time in his life, he began to think in moral and ethical terms.

Late in the spring of 1785, Wilberforce and Milner returned to Europe to accompany the women on their trip back home. As they drove down to the Mediterranean, the men read the New Testament (from the Bible) … in Greek. And on their return, they talked.

That fall of 1785, Wilberforce began a daily practice of reading the Bible and praying. And his religious concerns became so strong that, early in December, he decided to speak with the Rev. John Newton.[2] Newton was well known among the wealthy as a "religious enthusiast." And, as with Wilberforce's Aunt and Uncle Thornton, Newton was someone whom any self-respecting person would avoid at all costs. But for some reason Wilberforce never explained, he thought Newton could help him in some way.

---

2. Wilberforce had listened to Newton preach many times when he lived with his aunt and uncle. Newton had been a slave ship captain. i.e., he had helped to capture African men and women and then transport them from Africa to become slaves in the New World. At a certain point in his life, Newton decided to follow the teachings of Jesus. As a result, he gave up slaving and became a pastor. Nowadays, he is most famous for having written the hymn called "Amazing Grace."

When the day came for his visit, Wilberforce was so afraid of being seen going into the Rev. Newton's home that he walked around the block several times before he got up the nerve to knock on the door. By the time he left, he had decided to become what he called "a real Christian"—someone who followed the teachings of Jesus.

That evening, he decided to tell Pitt about what was on his mind. He wrote a brief letter to Pitt and said that he had devoted his life to God and was afraid their relationship would never be the same. Among the changes he said Pitt should plan for: "I expect soon to announce my resignation from the House."

Pitt was alarmed. "Please!" he wrote back. "I want to hear what you are thinking. And let us discuss your ideas before you make any final decision about your continued service in the House …"

Wilberforce agreed. And when the two men met, they were able to talk openly about their thoughts and feelings. Wilberforce didn't convince Pitt to become a Christian. But Pitt convinced Wilberforce not to leave politics—at least for the time being. "Give yourself some time to think things through," he said. And Wilberforce agreed to do that.

As it turned out, a few months later, Wilberforce was as great a presence in the House as he had ever been. But his relationship with Pitt changed. Though their personal values and commitments remained close, their motives differed. For instance, when Pitt needed to make a decision about a Bill, he always considered the good of the *country* and whether *voters* would like it. Wilberforce always asked a somewhat different set of questions: "Is this *right* [according to his understanding of the Bible]?"

"Is this what *God* wants?"

Both men soon realized that Wilberforce would vote his conscience no matter what anyone else said or did.[3] And because Pitt knew that Wilberforce would vote his conscience, he knew he could no longer speak as openly with Wilberforce as he once had. He no longer felt as comfortable as he once had to share with Wilberforce all the intimate details about the parliamentary tricks and inside deal-making he engaged in to get other MPs to vote with him on different matters.

Besides the changes in Wilberforce, Pitt, too, became a significantly different man in 1785. With all the responsibilities of Prime Minister, Pitt became busier than ever with government matters.

And so, from that point on, these two former best friends drifted apart. Though they remained very *friendly* one to the other, they never again acted quite as carefree and open with one another as they had before.

Question

1. Why did the relationship between Pitt and Wilberforce change in 1785?

---

3. As a result, Wilberforce became one of the first truly independent MPs in British history. He voted according to his own convictions, not according to any particular party's preference.

CHAPTER 5: A CHANGED MAN

After deciding to follow Jesus, Wilberforce quit all five of the private clubs he had joined—the clubs where he had spent so many nights laughing, drinking, playing cards and foining.

The people who knew him best sensed that he was more serious about life than he had been. But they had no idea how much his thoughts and feelings had changed.

All the pleasure he had once enjoyed when attending parties and dinners seemed to disappear. And how do we know? Because we can read his diary.

"How vain and foolish all the conversation of great dinners: nothing worth remembering," he wrote.

"Dined at Lord Chatham's. All the 'greats' present. How unbecoming this feels to me! How unnatural for one who professes himself a stranger and a pilgrim!" By contrast, then, there were comments like this: "Dined at home. Milner and I had some serious talk."

Despite his growing negative feelings, Wilberforce maintained positive relationships with those he had always spent time with in the past. He no longer tried to be the center of attention, but he did try to be a friend. And he participated in as much merry-making with his friends as he felt he could.

But he also began to do things that were more uniquely "Christian." For example, he began to bow his head to say a prayer before every meal. He also tried to "do good" for his friends—as he put it—by trying to turn their conversations to spiritual matters.

Unlike some "enthusiasts" who would turn their back in disgust on the kinds of people with whom he spent his time, Wilberforce always tried to be kindly, courteous, and engaging. Despite his good-natured kindness and courtesy, however, Wilberforce's mother expressed deep concern about her son's evangelical "madness" as she called it.[1]

Wilberforce was quieter and more reserved than he had been at one time, it was true. But he was more considerate and even-tempered than he had ever been as well.

Question

1. How did Wilberforce's life change after he became what he called "a real Christian"?

---

1. **Mad**, here, does not mean *angry*. It means *insane, crazy*.

CHAPTER 6: THE ABOLITIONIST CAUSE

In the early 1700s, a few people were beginning to believe that Slavery was morally wrong. As early as 1724, the Quakers[1] passed resolutions that stated their beliefs in this regard. In 1761, they passed a resolution that said no one could be a Quaker if they participated in the Slave Trade.

Primarily in response to the Quakers, but with the encouragement of some Wesleyans[2] as well, Parliament considered several Bills to abolish or severely cut back on the slave trade. But the House permitted every proposal to die without ever coming to a vote.

Many leading Quakers were frustrated by this lack of action. Finally, in 1787, several men decided to form a national Committee for the Abolition of the Slave Trade. Most Committee members were Quakers, but there were a few others as well.

The Committee set its first goal: To gather information about the horrors of the Slave Trade. Its second goal— and the reason for gathering the information: To make the people of England aware of the horrors. But if they wanted to achieve their ultimate goal and make the Slave Trade illegal, they realized they needed a friend in Parliament. They needed

- someone who would speak for them;
- someone who would act on principle rather than

---

1. The **Quakers**, officially known as the Society of Friends, were begun in 1647 by an Englishman named George Fox. Fox taught that true Christians have an "Inner Light," the light of Jesus' Spirit, inside them. Those who listen carefully can follow that light without anyone helping them. They didn't need ministers or priests or any other church leaders. Quakers have always rejected war (such people are called *pacifists*) and led in the Abolition of Slavery, prison reform, the humane treatment of mental patients, and other such causes.

2. **Wesleyans**, also known as Methodists (because their religious practices were very methodical), were "religious enthusiasts" who followed the teachings of John and Charles Wesley. See Footnote 1 on p. 3.

simply do what he thought would make voters happy;

- someone who would permit his name to be associated with the cause of Abolition no matter what the cost;
- someone who could speak forcefully yet winsomely;
- someone who had the personal strength and reputation in Parliament that he could make one motion, then another like it, and another and another—as many as might be required.

They needed someone who could present motions in such a way that they would not push the other MPs (Members of Parliament) away, but, instead, would hold their attention and even draw their interest.

They needed someone who could present the evidence and reasoning for the motions in such a way that the Members would realize how horrible the Trade was. But he had to be able to talk in such a way that they wouldn't feel as if he *enjoyed* making the Traders look bad.

And the Committee members realized that they needed to choose someone who had a good relationship with the Prime Minister. As we have seen, the Prime Minister made all the decisions about whether and how a Bill came before Parliament. If the Prime Minister opposed a Bill, he could make it almost impossible to get the Bill passed.

As they discussed these things, the Committee members realized William Wilberforce was the only man who met all their requirements. And so they asked him if he would help. They were thrilled when he said he would do everything he could to assist them.

Little did he realize what a large commitment he had just made!

Over the course of the next half year, Wilberforce

worked closely with members of the Committee. He consulted with his friend, Prime Minister Pitt. And he worked with other interested parties to gather as much evidence as he could about the Trade. He needed all this information to present to Parliament.

While only two or three years before you would have found Wilberforce spending half the night drinking, singing and dancing, now you could find him working with one or more of his friends. They would spend that time discussing the evidence they could present to Parliament. Pitt himself was very interested in the project and was as involved in the process as he could be considering all the other responsibilities he had as Prime Minister.

Wilberforce intended to present his Bill in February of 1788. But by mid-January, he and the Committee realized that if they were to present a convincing case, they needed to gather a few more pieces of evidence.

That was discouraging. But it got worse. By February, it looked as if Wilberforce might die. His digestive system had always been weak. But now he could barely eat. And what he did eat, he could not digest. He began to lose weight rapidly. By late March, his doctors said he would not live more than two weeks—three at the most.

Wilberforce called Pitt to his bedside. "Please," he asked his friend, "will you make the cause of the slaves your own?"

Pitt said he would do so gladly.[3]

As it turned out, Wilberforce was able to survive his intestinal attack and over the next several months he im-

---

3. Wilberforce made the request but he was astonished and grateful when Pitt agreed. The Abolitionist cause, he knew, was highly unpopular. If Pitt were to fulfill his promise to Wilberforce, it could easily cost him his position as Prime Minister, and it might also end his entire political career.

proved enough at least to begin writing letters and talking with people again. It was almost a year, however, before he was able to return to Parliament.

Questions

1. What was the Committee for the Abolition of the Slave Trade?

2. What kept Wilberforce from presenting his Bill when originally planned?

CHAPTER 7: THE FIRST PROPOSAL

While Wilberforce healed, Pitt fulfilled his promise to make the cause of the slaves his own. He made a motion[1] that the House should agree to study the Slave Trade early in 1789. Pitt carefully avoided suggesting what his own views were on the subject. All he said was that he thought the House should commit itself to study the subject.

After Pitt made his speech, Charles Fox, one of the leading members of Parliament, stood to speak. Both Pitt and Wilberforce had always thought Fox opposed them. "I would like to make it clear," he said, "that I believe the Trade ought not to be *regulated*. Rather, it should be *destroyed*!"

Pitt had merely proposed that the House should *study* and *talk about* the Trade. And he had said they should agree to do so *next year*. But Fox was ready not merely to *talk* but, obviously, to *do battle* against slavery. And he was ready to do it *right now* and *not* next year!

When Fox sat down, Edmund Burke, another leading member of the House, also spoke. And Burke, too, spoke in favor not merely of regulation, but of outright Abolition.[2] Other MPs spoke, and the majority seemed in favor of Abolition. Only one said anything in opposition. Abolition, said this one member, is "unnecessary and impractical."

Of course, Pitt had only asked the House to commit

---

1. To *make a motion* means to ask a legislative body (like the British Parliament) to agree on some proposal. When one brings a proposal for consideration, one says, "I move …" — and then one states what the proposal is — " … that the House should study the Slave Trade early in 1789."

2. *Abolition:* doing away with or putting a stop to something—in this case, putting an end to the slave trade and, though by no means clear, possibly even putting an end to slavery itself.

itself to *consider* the matter … in its next session. When the House finally voted on his proposal, the resolution passed without one vote opposing.

Something else occurred in 1788 while Wilberforce was absent.

On May 26, Sir William Dolben presented a Bill to limit the number of slaves a ship might carry. Dolben explained that he had gone onboard a slave ship lying at anchor. He had discovered, quite by accident, that slaves were being packed into that particular ship so closely, it was as if they were "books on a shelf." There was so little room on the ship, Dolben said, that a man could not lie on his back much less stretch himself.

MPs who supported the Trade were horrified that someone—Dolben—would talk about these things in public. Lord Penrhyn, for example, said, "It is absurd to suppose that men, whose profit depends on the health and strength of these African natives, would purposely treat them in a way that might endanger their lives."

But whether reasonable or not, during the debate, men who were involved in the Trade testified that many slaves *died* on the voyage from Africa to their final destination. Five to ten percent of slaves (in other words, 1 out of every 10 to 20) died on the *typical* voyage across the Atlantic. But in at least one case, more than a third of the slaves had died.

With these kinds of admissions, it became obvious that the Trade's spokespeople were lying when they claimed that "the voyage from Africa is the happiest period of the slave's life!"

By this point in the debate, the Trade became desperate. "If Parliament regulates us in any way," they said, "our entire business will be ruined. Furthermore, every slave passed over by British ships will simply be transported by the French …" In other words, not only will you lose tax revenues, but our enemies—the French—will become wealthy.

These arguments were obviously made in the Slavers' own personal interests. And they showed an obvious lack of concern for justice. As a result, they didn't fare well in the Commons. Instead, the arguments spurred some MPs to action—men who had previously been unconcerned about slavery. When Dolben's Bill to limit the number of slaves that a ship could carry finally came to a vote, it passed, 56 to 5.

Still, it could not become law unless the House of Lords approved as well. The Trade had more support in Lords than it did in Commons. Indeed, it appeared that the Bill would face certain defeat. At that point, Pitt threw his entire weight behind it.

"If this Bill should be defeated," Pitt declared, "I will no longer remain in the same Cabinet as those who opposed it." In other words, he was saying, he was willing to risk all of his power, his entire position in government, on this one issue. If he lost and the Bill was defeated, he had said he was willing to be thrown out of power. Such a position was both bold and risky. But it put his Cabinet on notice that he was deadly serious about getting his way.

When the Bill finally came to a vote, it passed Lords by two votes: 14 to 12.

With the passage of Pitt's resolution to consider the Trade in 1789, and now with Dolben's regulations in place, those who were involved in the Trade knew that they needed to be prepared for an attack. Their interests were in danger. They had been making money hand over fist, but with Dolben's Bill and, now, the possibility of further limitations, their profits could be reduced.

And so, the Slave Trade used public meetings, newspaper articles, and dozens of pamphlets to argue that, without the Trade, the British economy would be ruined. Further, while Abolition would cripple England, it would do no good for the slaves, either. For one thing, they said, the Trade is nothing like what the Abolitionists claim. The Abolitionists don't know what they are talking about. They have never been on board a slave ship. They have never been to the West Indies. And they know nothing of what Slavery is really all about.

And beyond everything else, one pamphlet argued, those who are being enslaved *deserve* to be enslaved. If anything, their enslavement is a positive *benefit* to them. It preserves them from a *worse* fate in their native lands.

Questions

1. Lord Penrhyn said, "It is absurd to suppose that men, whose profit depends on the health and strength of these African natives, would purposely treat them in a way that might endanger their lives." What do you think is a good response to such a statement?

2. What did Pitt do in order to get the Lords to pass Dolben's Bill?

CHAPTER 8: THE BATTLE IS JOINED

In the midst of the Slave Trade's campaign, on May 12, 1789, William Wilberforce finally stood to "ask the question" in the House of Commons. He proposed twelve resolutions. The resolutions would declare that Parliament disapproved of a number of specific evils associated with the Trade. Further, they would declare Parliament's intention that the trade in African *slaves* should be replaced by trade in African *goods*.

Wilberforce presented his resolutions. Then he spoke for three and a half hours to explain and argue for them. At the end of his presentation, and as soon as he sat down, the Speaker of the House offered his support. Then Pitt stood to offer his. Fox followed Pitt.

Pitt said that Wilberforce's resolutions were logical and just. Fox appealed to the MPs' emotions. He shared concrete examples of what Slavery looked like.

He told the story of a runaway slave who had been caught and brought back to the plantation from which he had run. As punishment for his crime, and to keep him from fleeing again, his master called upon a surgeon to cut off one of his legs. The surgeon refused. And so the master broke the slave's leg.

Fox told other stories as well. Another slave owner, he said, had taken a young female slave and tied her to a wooden beam by the wrists. As she hung there, defenseless, he prodded and poked her with burning brands.

"I ask, Sir," said Fox, "how we would feel if captured and carried away by a tribe as savage as our countrymen show themselves to be?"

The arguments and appeals made by these four

speakers, Wilberforce, Burke, Pitt and Fox, made an obvious impact on their hearers. But now it was time for the advocates for the Trade to defend themselves.

They came well prepared.

One MP said that Wilberforce had given the wrong impression about the situation. The Trade is not nearly as bad as Wilberforce has made it appear, he said. The slaves are really very happy in their conditions. "I have often expressed the wish that English workers might be half as happy as the black slaves."

Stronger arguments followed.

"There is no reason to feel sorry for these people," said another MP. "This is a hard world and, obviously, the weak suffer in it. We cannot right all wrongs, and we cannot allow ourselves to be controlled by emotional appeals to vague ideas of 'humanity.' That weak people must suffer for their weakness is simply part of the world order ..."

Others were more practical. They expressed concern for the British businessmen and slave owners who might suffer losses if Parliament were to do anything to change the rules concerning the slave trade.

"Should the Trade be abolished," said one, "it will mean the downfall of Britain, certainly the loss of all our colonies ..."

"Merchants who have risked their all in ships that have already sailed will be ruined by a decision of this magnitude," argued another.

"The passage of such a Bill will lead to a mass uprising on the part of the slaves," warned a third.

Then, too, there was that matter of national pride and well-being: "Every slave not taken by English ships will be taken by the French, and we know what that will mean in terms of their wealth and ours ..."

Finally, someone said, whatever God might demand in terms of justice for the slaves, we are talking about "the property of the West Indians.[1] And though we may be generous with our own property, we should not be generous with the property of others."

"Are numbers of Englishmen to be suddenly deprived of what the law allows them to possess? Are we to deprive them of their livelihood? Unpleasant as it may be, public opinion has permitted them to pursue their Trade for many years. And we in Parliament have at least tacitly given them permission ... ."

The arguments of the anti-Abolition forces were strong, and many of the MPs felt their weight. Wilberforce, Burke, Pitt and Fox had argued with great moral force. Their selflessness was obvious. So was the *self*-interest of the pro-Slavery forces. But the members of Parliament were unwilling to make a decision.

Finally, an MP who had remained silent stood. "Sir," he said, addressing the Chair in the customary manner. "The evidence presented in favor of this motion was gathered not by members of this House, but by the King's Privy Council. If we should adopt this motion on the basis of evidence gathered by that body, we shall have forever relinquished our right to require an independent investigation by this House ... . I believe that such a precedent is both dangerous and unnecessary. Therefore, rather than voting on the matter before us, I move that we establish a committee from this House whose task

---

1. *West Indians:* People—and in this case, especially British subjects—who live in the islands on the east edge of the Caribbean Sea and the western North Atlantic (i.e., the Bahamas and the Turk & Caicos Islands).

shall be to gather evidence concerning the Slave Trade ..."

With this proposal, the tension in the House collapsed. The proposal could postpone a final decision on this great moral issue forever, and no one would have to be embarrassed. And so the House abandoned its discussion of the Slave Trade.

Questions

1. Summarize the arguments both for and against Abolition of the Slave Trade.

2. What observation finally determined what the House was going to do with Wilberforce's motion? Why did this matter?

CHAPTER 9: PROLONGING THE DISCUSSION

A few weeks after the House of Commons voted to establish an investigative committee, Wilberforce was asked to lead it. The committee included eight or nine regular members. Other MPs who wanted to participate were invited to participate whenever the committee held a hearing.

And so the investigation began.

The committee offered the pro-Slavery forces the first opportunity to present evidence. And they provided witnesses. But at the same time, the pro-Slavery members did everything possible to slow the hearings. They seemed determined to cause as much frustration and boredom as possible. The committee members could tell that the pro-Slavery group hoped to make the committee's hearings so awful that the House might cancel the hearings altogether. Eventually, however, the committee was able to listen to all of the pro-Slavery evidence and so they turned to the Abolitionists and offered them the opportunity to present their case.

As soon as that happened, suddenly, the Slave interests demanded a quick vote.

"I believe we have heard enough evidence," said one pro-Slavery MP. "Clearly, the House must be convinced that Abolition is impractical. Further evidence, therefore, is unnecessary and will simply cause delay … . So let the House give a decisive vote right away and put an end to these dangerous discussions!"

Other members, however, knew it was only fair to permit the Abolitionists to present their case. They should have just as much right to present their evidence as the pro-Slavery side had enjoyed.

And the Abolitionists were fully ready to present their evidence. So they began their testimony. Beyond their testimony to the committee directly, they also launched a campaign to make their case to the British people at large.

Since most British subjects had never seen a slave and knew little if anything about the way slaves were forced to live (let alone how they were made slaves in the first place), the Abolitionists determined to educate them. Then the Abolitionists appealed to their listeners to make their voices heard.

As a result of the Abolitionists' efforts, Britain was soon flooded with pamphlets, popular songs, and even jewelry designed to urge Abolition of the Trade. The Abolitionist cause became a very popular one. Some people boycotted West Indian (i.e., *slave-produced*) sugar. By their actions, they showed they would willingly suffer with the slaves until Parliament finally voted against the Trade. These boycotters also wanted to put pressure on the slave owners by reducing their income.

Figure 1 - The image of a supplicant male slave in chains adapted from the seal of the British Society for the Abolition of Slavery. The image appeared on several medallions for the society made as early as 1787. This particular woodcut appeared 50 years later—on an 1837 American publication of poet John Greenleaf Whittier's anti-slavery poem, "Our Countrymen in Chains!"
Image courtesy of the Library of Congress.

Besides all these activities, the Abolitionists circulated petitions. On April 2, 1792, when Wilberforce made a speech on the floor of Parliament and again moved that the Slave Trade should be abolished, he presented 499 petitions and almost a million signatures that all declared support for his cause. The slave owners presented just five petitions with signatures of people who wanted to support the Slave Trade.

Dundas, one of the senior members of the House, stood immediately after Wilberforce concluded his speech. "I fully agree with the goals Mr. Wilberforce has laid before us," he said. "However, I propose that we seek the same ends by *regulating* the Trade rather than abolishing it outright ..."

Fox was furious. "And what regulations would the gentleman propose?" he roared.

Dundas was ready: "Regulations that will promote the breeding of negroes in the West Indies so that there is no more need for importation. Regulations that will put an end, gradually, to hereditary slavery. Regulations that will improve the conditions of existing slaves. And regulations that will provide for the education of their children," he replied.

Dundas then turned to face the House: "I appeal to all gentlemen of the moderate or middle way of thinking to avoid the extreme policies and associated dangers of Mr. Wilberforce's proposal ..."

Fox could not contain his anger. "The idea of 'moderation' in the Slave Trade," he thundered, "reminds me of the suggestion that 'To break into a man's house and kill him, his wife, and his family in the night is certainly an awful crime, but even this may be done with moderation'! ... The real question is not whether that disgusting Trade requires *regulation*, but whether it is fit to be *continued at all!*" He calmed himself and then concluded: "It seems to me, Sir, that by proposing regulation, Mr. Dundas is seeking to lay a foundation for preserving this Trade ... and not merely for years but forever ..."

It was now Dundas' turn to interrupt: "Rather than prolonging the debate, let me propose a simple amendment," he suggested. "Let us insert the word 'gradually' in Mr. Wilberforce's motion. I believe the value of my proposal will be obvious to any level-headed gentlemen."

And so it was that, on April 3, 1792, at 7 in the morning, having debated all night, Britain's House of Commons adopted Dundas' amendment by a vote of 193-125, and Wilberforce's motion, as amended, 230-85. The Slave Trade was to be abolished "gradually."

But what does *gradually* mean? Wilberforce wanted to know. How would Parliament measure its proposed "gradual" abolition?

After having debated all night, no one in the House was prepared to answer these questions. But the members of the House walked out into the morning sunshine having at least *implied* that the Slave Trade was wrong even if they hadn't yet decided exactly what to do about it.

Questions

1. After the initial debate (described in the previous chapter), the MPs who spoke in behalf of the Trade stopped arguing so much and instead engaged in other tactics to stop the Abolitionists. What tactics did they use?

2. Dundas made two major proposals. What were they?

3. Why do you think Dundas' proposals could seem good to both people who were *opposed* to the Slave Trade as well as to those who were in *favor* of the Trade?

CHAPTER 10: THE MIDDLE PASSAGE

Wilberforce was unwilling to let the House get away with its vague statement about gradual abolition. He demanded to know what, specifically, that word "gradual" meant. Three and a half weeks later, on April 27, 1792, he received his answer. The House agreed that the word "gradual" meant four years in the future. The Slave Trade—the capture and transport of African slaves—was to end by 1796 ... unless it proved too difficult.[1]

Having now voted to gradually abolish the Slave Trade, and having defined the word "gradually," the House of Commons then passed its Bill on to the House of Lords. This time it was the Lords who used the tactic that had been used in the Commons three years before. The Lords delayed the Bill so they could "collect evidence." Too bad they never gathered any! And so, as a result, the Lords never voted on the Bill ... and the Bill died of neglect.

Despite the ultimate death of his Bill, Wilberforce determined to try again.

In February of 1793, England went to war with France. When a country goes to war, the legislative branch will usually push all other concerns to the end of the agenda. Despite the war, Wilberforce stood to make a motion for gradual Abolition. As we have already seen, Dundas' almost identical motion the previous year had passed by a wide margin. But in 1793, it was defeated.

How discouraging!

But Wilberforce was not to be turned aside.

Later that year he thought he might be able to

---

1. But what does "too difficult" mean? Like "gradually," "too difficult" is a weasel phrase. It pretends to say something when it doesn't say anything at all. Do you see the problem? The government might do almost nothing and say: "Oh! It's too difficult!"

limit the Slave Trade by prohibiting British ships from transporting slaves for sale in foreign countries. So Wilberforce proposed a Bill to that effect.

His "Foreign Slave Bill" was defeated by two votes.

In the next few paragraphs, I am going to tell you only the barest details of what Wilberforce did—for years: year after year. Recounting these few details in such a short space will almost certainly give you the wrong impression. You will feel as if all Wilberforce had to do was stand up, say a few words, sit down, then wait a year to do the same thing once more. The truth is far more complicated. You should keep in mind that what Wilberforce did in all of these years was at least as difficult as what I have told you in the last four chapters. Every year. And Wilberforce himself—and those who supported him—faced not just ridicule, but real danger to themselves and their families. Those who opposed them did so not only with rational arguments in Parliament, but with threats and actions that put the Abolitionists in physical danger and fear of real harm.

I will not recount those details. Just know that the details could be told. The *outline* of Wilberforce's political movement can be summarized as follows.

In **1794**, Wilberforce proposed another Foreign Slave Bill. This one passed the Commons by 18 votes. But no one was willing to bring it up for a vote in the House of Lords!

Two years later, in **1796**—the year by which the Commons had agreed the Trade should be abolished—Wilberforce was finally able to bring forward another Bill for debate.

Things looked bright for the motion … until the night when the final vote was to be taken.

Dundas gave six or seven of Wilberforce's supporters free tickets to attend the opening night performance of a new opera. And so Dundas was present while Wilberforce's friends were not. And Wilberforce's motion was defeated by a vote of 70 to 74.

In **1797**, Wilberforce lost by a vote of 74 to 82.

In **1798**, the vote was 83 to 87.

In **1799**, 54 to 84.

In 1800, Wilberforce didn't propose a Bill because the slave owners implied that they were willing to negotiate a settlement. Nothing came of their proposal, however, so four years later, in **1804**, Wilberforce made a new motion.

Astonishingly, it passed Commons by a vote of 124 to 49. Victory looked so close!

But as had occurred in 1792, the Bill was defeated in the House of Lords. The Lords actually voted on it this time, but four royal dukes took the lead in opposing the measure.

It was to be at least another year before Wilberforce could push the issue again.

In **1805**, Wilberforce lost once more. His Bill was defeated in Commons by a vote of 70 to 77.

Talk about discouraging! Where had all the votes from 1804 gone?

As if the vote in 1805 had not been bad enough, by Christmas, Pitt was deathly ill.

And in January 1806, Pitt died. Wilberforce lost the one who had supported him more faithfully and effectively than any others through all the years he had been in Parliament.

Questions

1. Pitt died in January 1806. This was how many years after the Committee to Abolish the Slave Trade had asked Wilberforce to champion their cause?

2. Counting the Bills he presented in 1789 and 1792 (as well as all the ones mentioned in this chapter), how many Bills did Wilberforce present to Parliament in order to limit or Abolish the Trade?

3. Why would Pitt's death have been discouraging to Wilberforce?

CHAPTER 11: THE END GAME

After 18 years of defeat and now with his best friend, one of the most powerful men in all of Britain, dead, the future looked bleak for Wilberforce.

It was then that James Stephen, Wilberforce's brother-in-law, suggested a bold and creative idea. He caught Wilberforce in the hall just an hour before Wilberforce planned to make his annual motion against the Trade.

"Look here," said Stephen. "Remember Pitt's Order in Council last September? We always emphasized how it forbade importing slaves into Dutch New Guinea. But it went further, remember? It forbade British ships from carrying slaves to *any* foreign territory. It also forbade them from bringing slaves to *newly acquired* British territories. And, lastly, it forbade outfitting foreign slave ships in British ports. But the slaveholders were perfectly happy."[1]

"Yes," said Wilberforce. "I remember."

"Well," Stephen continued, "it is normal for an Order in Council to be confirmed by a Bill in Parliament. The slave interests were delighted with Pitt's Order, and I think they would support a Bill to *extend* the Order ... since it protects their interests against foreign competition. But, from *our* perspective, it would, for the first time, place Parliament in a position of *limiting* and not merely *regulating* the Trade ..."

Wilberforce's eyes shone with pleasure. "That is a *wonderful* idea!" he exclaimed.

---

1. Dutch New Guinea had been captured by Britain but everyone expected the Dutch to take control once more. The territory had never had slaves, but if England permitted them, then slaves would remain in the territory even after the Dutch took them over. No one in England wanted to have foreign territories opened to Slavery. Even the slaveholders were opposed to such an idea. They recognized that additional slave territories would mean greater competition for their own products.

He withheld making his motion that evening. Instead, he and Stephen carefully laid new plans and, when they presented their Bill, it floated through Parliament more smoothly than even Stephen had imagined. Virtually no one opposed it.

Having achieved a first *limitation* on the Trade, Wilberforce, Stephen and other Abolitionists—including the new Prime Minister, Lord Grenville—worked together on the next step.

Rather than have Wilberforce introduce another Bill in the Commons, they agreed to have Grenville introduce a Bill in the House of Lords! The entire approach could lead to a new outcome. By having Grenville introduce it, the Bill would enjoy a tremendous advantage because it would be a Government issue.[2]

On January 2, 1807, the Prime Minister, Lord Grenville, moved in the House of Lords his "Bill for the Abolition of the Slave Trade." The most important provision was this one: after May 1st, 1807, the African Slave Trade and "all manner of dealing and Trading in the purchase of slaves or their transport from Africa to the West Indies or any other territory is utterly abolished, prohibited and declared to be unlawful." Beyond that: any British ship found to be involved in the Trade would immediately become property of the Crown.[3]

The motion was delayed for several months, but when debate finally got underway, it passed the Lords by a majority of 64 votes. In the Commons, the Foreign Secretary introduced the Bill. Many others gave their

---

2. ***Government issue:*** The Prime Minister and his cabinet, in Britain, are called "the Government." If "the Government" proposes a matter, it means that the Prime Minister is saying, as Pitt had said concerning his motion back in 1788: "If this Bill fails, I am willing to lose my job over it. I am willing to disband Parliament and call for new national elections."

3. ***The Crown:*** the royal government.

hearty approval. Only two people spoke against it.

The capstone of the "debate" (which wasn't really a debate at all) occurred when the Attorney General spoke. Rather than addressing the Bill itself, he turned to praise Wilberforce. "When I consider the feelings that will accompany my honorable friend after tonight's vote," he began … –He was never permitted to finish his sentence.

Round after round of cheers filled the House. Wilberforce sat with his head in his hands, tears streaming down his face. Could it actually be? Was it possible that his dream—Pitt's dream, the dream of so many of his friends—would actually be fulfilled this night, some 20 years after the Committee for the Abolition of the Slave Trade had first formed? It seemed impossible. But minutes later he had his answer.

The House voted in favor of the Bill by a resounding 283 to 16!

Later that evening, joking with a friend, Wilberforce laughed: "Well, Henry, what shall we abolish next?" Someone else remarked: "What shall we do with those 16 villains who voted against us?"

"Never mind the miserable 16," Wilberforce replied. "Think of the glorious 283!"

Sir James Mackintosh, when he heard of the vote, wrote to congratulate Wilberforce from Bombay, India. "We are apt to express wonder that so much exertion should be necessary to stop such awful injustices," he said. "We ought, rather, to marvel that it would take but the short span of one man's life to remedy the miseries of millions for ages."

* * *

People wonder why and how Wilberforce was able to

pursue the issue so persistently year after year. In 1793, he wrote to a friend: "Where a real moral evil is in question, someone who fears God is not at liberty to waver. Even if I thought that the immediate Abolition of the Slave Trade would cause a revolution in our islands, I would not stop what I am doing. Be persuaded, then, if I would not stop because of revolution, I am far less concerned about political convenience or personal feeling."

Questions

1. What did Stephen mean when he said that his proposal would "place Parliament in a position of limiting and not merely regulating the Trade ..."? What is the difference between *limiting* and *regulating*?

2. What does it mean to say that something is "a Government issue"?

3. Explain Sir James Mackintosh's statement that "We ought ... to marvel that it would take but the short span of one man's life to remedy the miseries of millions for ages." What was he saying?

CHAPTER 12: EPILOGUE ON THE SLAVE TRADE

William Wilberforce is best remembered for his work in abolishing the Slave Trade. But even though the British government made it illegal to sell and transport slaves, that did not mean that the British slave traders stopped their activities. And it didn't encourage any other nations to take action. Most importantly, it did nothing to free any of those who were already enslaved.

The King of Denmark had actually preceded Britain in declaring that "all traffic in the Slave Trade by our subjects shall cease." He did that effective January 1, 1803. But other countries—most notably France, Spain, Portugal, and the United States—maintained and even expanded their involvement in the Trade.

So Wilberforce and his friends put pressure on the British government to do what it could to suppress the Trade. First, in 1807, immediately after their Bill passed, they convinced the government to send a squadron of warships to find and capture illegal British traders. Two years later, in 1809, they pressured the government to authorize the Navy to search Portuguese ships for slave cargoes.

In 1810, again at Wilberforce's bidding, Britain paid the Portuguese government to forbid Portuguese slavers from trading anywhere in Africa that was not actually owned by Portugal. Also, the same year, Parliament increased its pressure on British Slavers by making trade in slaves a felony.[1]

Still the Trade continued. So, with Wilberforce taking the lead in Parliament, the Abolitionists maintained

---

1. *Felony:* a serious crime; one punishable by death or by imprisonment for more than a year.

pressure on the government to do whatever it could to end the Trade. At one point, they were able to get a sixth of the entire British Navy involved in pursuing the Slavers.

Finally, Wilberforce and his friends were able to push through a Bill that required all slaves to be counted and identified. That permitted the government to detect if, when, and where slaves were being smuggled into the West Indies.

In the meantime, however, the Abolitionists were enraged as the Trade ignored and obstructed the law. Even more, they were angered by the stories they heard about the cruel treatment endured by those who already were slaves.

There was the story of the slave owner who sentenced two brothers to 100 lashes each because someone claimed they had accepted a pair of stolen stockings. When the brothers were whipped, their sister cried. She, then, was sentenced to receive 30 lashes because she had cried.

Another slave who had run away from his master was caught. He was returned to his master and his master beat him mercilessly. Immediately after the beating, the master then chained the slave to another man so that the two could work together. The man who had been beaten complained of pain and hunger. When he sat down, the estate manager had him whipped some more until he stood up. Later that day, he died. He was still chained to his companion.

When news of this event reached Britain, there was a public outcry. The estate manager was eventually tried, convicted of manslaughter,[2] and given a sentence of 90 days in jail and a fine of £200.

By making these cases known to the British people, the Abolitionists gained more and more people who were willing to speak out against the whole institution of Slavery.

The slaveholders themselves, however, had some weapons to use against the Abolitionists. One wrote an "open letter" to Wilberforce concerning a pamphlet Wilberforce had written.

"Your book is a great deal of trash," wrote the slaveholder. "It is a great deal of lying and a great deal of cool falsehood for which the Quakers are famed .... Any man who knows anything at all of the real situation of the Blacks will declare you totally ignorant of the subject and a perfect hypocrite .... You seem to have great affection for the fat, lazy, laughing and singing negroes while you ignore the plight of the wage slaves who surround you on every hand .... Never have you done one single act in favor of the laborers of this country ...."

As time passed, Abolitionists began to realize that as long as the institution of Slavery itself remained legal, there would be too strong a demand for slaves and far too few limitations on the violence and cruelty of wicked masters. It was not enough merely to stop the Slave Trade. Britain needed to abolish the entire institution of Slavery.

Wilberforce, by this point, was too old to take a strong and active role. His name and his influence remained, but someone else had to take the lead.

---

2. People who commit ***manslaughter*** have killed someone, but did so in circumstances that make the law view the killing as something less bad than murder. If you have murdered someone, it means you killed the person with malicious intent: you *wanted* to kill the person and you acted deliberately to cause the victim to die. By contrast, you might be convicted of manslaughter if you caused the death by accident.

Question

1. Why did the Abolitionists come to the conclusion that it was not enough merely to abolish the Slave Trade, but they had to abolish the entire institution of Slavery?

CHAPTER 13: SECRETS OF AN EFFECTIVE WORLD-CHANGER

Wilberforce not only affected the Slave Trade. He also deeply influenced British society as a whole.

How and why was he able to influence so many people?

One of his secrets was his attention to detail. He took the time to gather the information he needed and to organize his arguments so that he could sway his audience. Further, he always tried to think of comments he could make or questions he could ask that might turn the conversation to the subjects that concerned him.

But Wilberforce's greatest strength was the fact that he truly and deeply *cared* for the people with whom he talked. He might be violently against what someone was saying—and Wilberforce never hesitated to state his own views on a subject!—but he went to great lengths to treat his opponents with respect and honor.

Thomas Buxton, who led the Abolitionist cause after Wilberforce retired, commented that, "Often during a debate, [Wilberforce] would whisper to me hints and witticisms that would have filled the House with laughter. They would have overwhelmed the opponent. But whenever he rose to speak, though he would say things very close to the thoughts he had poured into my ear, he restrained himself from uttering them. And he would never say something that might cause another pain."

Clearly, his mind was as sharp and his verbal skills were as powerful as when he had foined as a young man. But after he committed himself to follow the teachings of Jesus, Wilberforce never tried to put others down by showing how smart he was or how superior. He tried, instead, to convince them of better things. He sought to do this with gentleness, humility, kindness and humor.

It is often the case when people hold strong opinions that, without saying a word, they offend others. Their very presence offends and causes discomfort to the people around them. Wilberforce was usually able to avoid this problem.

He did this, first, by refusing to look down his nose on other people's weaknesses and failings. Second, he took care to show genuine interest in the people around him. He asked them thoughtful questions and he listened carefully to their answers.

His fellow guests at a dinner party would sometimes embarrass themselves and apologize to him for their bad language, but they never felt condemned by him. As a result, they never felt they should quit asking him to come to their parties. One person commented that when Wilberforce walked in late for a dinner, not a single person in the entire group frowned or made a negative comment. Instead, all the guests beamed with delight. His presence made them happy.

After having met with Wilberforce, the novelist Fanny Burney told her father that the hours she spent with him were "four hours of the best conversation I have ever enjoyed. His comments were all so thoughtful, so spirited, so full of information, yet so humble. I felt I was his confidential friend. I was really and truly delighted and enlightened by him."

Another woman confessed: "I have always heard that he is the most religious, but now I know that he is the wittiest man in England."

It seems Wilberforce took to heart the advice he

received from his friend Hannah More. Shortly after he decided to follow Jesus, she wrote: "You are serving God if you are courteous and pleasant to irreligious but friendly people. They would never be attracted to religion by critical and harsh clergymen."

By contrast, she wrote, "Your happy ways serve as an honest bait by which these people may be awakened to realize that you have not been driven to religion for lack of pleasure in life!"

After he became a Christian, Wilberforce stayed away from the theater and avoided playing cards or dancing, but he seemed never to think of condemning someone else for doing such things. As far as he was concerned, his beliefs and behavior were not things of which to be proud; rather, they were a gift from God.

But despite his pleasant and winsome manner, Wilberforce couldn't always avoid causing offense. One time he visited a nobleman who was dying. During the course of their conversation, Wilberforce never mentioned any religious topic.

Yet while they were talking, a friend of the dying man came into the room. "How are you?" the friend asked.

"Well enough," said the old man, "considering Wilberforce is sitting here telling me I am going to Hell."

Questions

1. List at least four things Wilberforce did that enabled him to influence other people.

2. Wilberforce obviously held strong opinions about religion, slavery, and other topics. But he seemed, generally, not to offend people. How did he avoid offending people?

3. No matter how winsome you may be, it is almost impossible not to cause offense to some people (as Wilberforce apparently did to the old nobleman). Why is that?

CHAPTER 14: FAMILY LIFE

Wilberforce married Barbara Spooner, the 20-year old daughter of a merchant and banker, on May 30, 1797, a few months before he turned 38. The two had first met only six weeks earlier, on April 15th.

Friends often wondered about Wilberforce's choice of a wife, but Wilberforce always said he enjoyed "a happiness at home beyond what could have been conceived possible."

The Wilberforces had six children.

One gets some sense of their home life through the descriptions of friends, family, and acquaintances. One of Wilberforce's distant cousins wrote,

> Barbara was extremely good looking and in some ways very clever. But she was very deficient in common sense. She held narrow views and idolized her husband to the point where she believed everything in the world ought to give way to what she thought best for him.
>
> Instead of making his home attractive to the crowds of upper-class people that he invited, Barbara's desire to save money made her anything but a hospitable hostess. Yet the strange appearances of what went on there often made up, especially to young people, for any faults.

It is quite clear that Barbara kept Wilberforce from going to all the public and social events he might otherwise have attended. But her fussiness may have helped prolong his life. He always struggled with his health.[1]

Many of the Wilberforce family's friends commented on Barbara's poor housekeeping. Wilberforce himself was a poor manager of his home. Where other wealthy

---

1. While Wilberforce had a beautiful and strong voice, his body was quite weak. He had extremely poor eyesight, and his bowels bothered him constantly. Several times in his life—not just the one time I recorded here—his doctors feared he would die. Several times during his life, he was laid up for months with intestinal problems.

families would keep a tight rein on their servants and household helpers, the Wilberforces permitted almost any standard that the servants chose for themselves.

The family had 13 or 14 servants. That was about average for a family of their size and standing in society. But the Wilberforces seemed to hire and keep servants not because the servants did their jobs well, but simply because it felt good ... or seemed easier than doing something else.

One cousin noted that "The house is thronged with servants who are kept on the payroll solely to be nice: an ex-secretary has been retained because W is 'grateful.' The ex-secretary's wife is still being paid because 'she nursed poor Barbara.' And there is an old butler who they wish would not stay but, they say, 'He is so attached.' And then there is the butler's wife who used to be a cook but now 'she is so infirm.'" So all of them remained on the payroll even though they contributed nothing to the current operation of the house.

Breakfasts at the Wilberforce home almost always included guests, and not just a few of them. As Hannah More once commented (with tongue obviously planted firmly in cheek): "Mr. Wilberforce is such a private person that he does not see more than 33 people at breakfast."[2]

The guests were not only numerous, they were so diverse that, as she put it, you could have mistaken them for "Noah's ark, full of beasts, clean and unclean."

You would find missionaries, politicians, people hoping to receive donations for one cause or another, even foreign diplomats. They might all be present at the table at the same time. Few if any of them could have

---

2. The original, unedited expression is funnier, if you can make out the words: "Mr. Wilberforce lives in such domestic retirement that he does not see above three and thirty people at breakfast."

possibly experienced a similar event anywhere else for the rest of their lives.

One of the guests at a breakfast described it in these terms: "Everyone was expected to fend for themselves. Mr. W was so shortsighted he could see nothing beyond his own plate. As a result, Mrs. W took care to supply him with all he wanted. Then Mr. Milner's voice was heard roaring, 'There is nothing on earth to eat!' Then asking the servants to bring some bread and butter, Milner added, 'And bring plenty without limit!' And Mr. W joined in with, 'Thank you. Thank you kindly, Milner, for seeing to these things. Mrs. W is not strong enough to meddle much in the way the house is run.'"

Garth Lean gives us one more picture of the Wilberforce household:

> Though men of Wilberforce's social status seldom spent time with their children, Wilberforce … loved to play with them. He ended a letter, "I am being called to play a game of marbles." More commonly, he played blind man's buff[3] or cricket.[4] …
>
> Wilberforce was delighted to have his children nearby. A friend was with him one day when, with rising frustration, Wilberforce was searching for a letter he had lost. Just then the clamor from the children's room above became overwhelming. The friend thought that now, at last, Wilberforce would give way to irritation. Instead, he paused, and with a delighted smile he said, "Only think what a relief, amidst other concerns, to hear their voices and know they are well!"

---

3. *Blind man's buff* [or "bluff"]: a form of tag in which "It" is blindfolded.

4. *Cricket:* a popular British bat-and-ball game.

Questions

1. Describe the Wilberforce family's manner of life.

2. What do you like about the way the Wilberforces lived?[5]

3. What do you dislike about their manner of living? (How would you do things differently?)

---

5. There is no "answer key" for this or the next question. I expect you to answer them for yourself.

CHAPTER 15: THE END OF THE STORY

By 1821, Wilberforce was in constant ill-health, and knew he needed a replacement to carry the Abolitionist battle forward. His wife had urged him for years to retire from public life. In May of 1821, he asked Thomas Buxton to take the lead in the anti-Slavery movement, but he didn't retire. In fact, two years later, in March of 1823, Wilberforce stood to introduce a petition for Parliament to free all the slaves by purchasing them from their masters. The motion was never debated and never voted on. And, as it turned out, it was the last Bill Wilberforce proposed in Parliament.

From that time forward, Buxton took the lead, and he followed the practice that Wilberforce had pioneered so many years before. Every year he presented another motion to free the slaves. Parliament never acted on Buxton's motions. But as he spoke and as his motions were at least briefly considered each year, he and the other Abolitionists in Parliament kept the Abolitionist cause before the House and did what they could to demonstrate that Slavery was truly awful.

By February of 1825, Wilberforce was so ill that he finally took Barbara's advice. He resigned from Parliament.

Five years later, in 1830, a General Election was held. Wilberforce's county, Yorkshire, had grown to the point where it had the right to elect not just two, but four MPs. And all four were Abolitionists. Clearly, the tide was turning.

By 1832, the Abolitionist members began to publish the names of candidates they considered "Anti-Abolition," "Doubtful," and "Recommended." The publication of these lists increased the number of Abolitionists in the House.

When a newly-elected Parliament first sat, it was a tradition for the King to address the assembly. During these speeches, he would tell Parliament what issues he believed were most important and what things he most wanted them to work on. In 1833, the King followed this tradition. In his speech, he said nothing about Slavery.

As soon as Buxton realized what had happened, he stood and gave notice that he intended to bring a motion concerning Slavery. The Prime Minister was alarmed. He went to Buxton privately and urged him to drop the matter. Buxton refused.

After a prolonged argument, the Prime Minister finally admitted defeat. "Well then," he said, "if you will not back down, then we [the Government[1]] must." And so he set a date on which the Government would express its views on the matter and on which a full debate could take place.

In preparing for the upcoming debate, the Abolitionists circulated pamphlets and asked for petitions. They held meetings and sponsored lectures all over the country.

In the midst of this activity, Wilberforce was asked to sign a petition. He was also invited to attend a meeting. He was more than 73 years old and extremely frail, but he agreed to go. Once he arrived at the meeting, though he had often declared that his speaking days were over, someone convinced him to take the floor.

One observer said that Wilberforce was so frail and his body so twisted that he seemed to sink right into his

---

1. Remember what "the Government" means: In Britain, the Prime Minister and his cabinets are called "the Government." If "the Government" proposes a matter, it means that the Prime Minister is saying: "If this Bill fails, I am willing to lose my job over it."

cloak. His voice, too, was only a faint shadow of what it had been 30, 40, or 50 years before. But somehow the passion of the old warrior came through.

Years earlier, when Wilberforce had been in his first term as an MP, Boswell, a famous commentator, had heard Wilberforce speak. Afterward, Boswell wrote, "I saw what seemed a mere shrimp [rise to speak]; but, as I listened, he grew, and grew, until the shrimp became a whale." That is how it had been in March of 1784. The same happened again in April of 1833, almost 50 years later.

"I had never thought to appear in public again," said Wilberforce. "But it shall never be said that William Wilberforce is silent while the slaves require his help."

And so he affirmed that the institution of Slavery should be abolished: "I say, and I say honestly and fearlessly, that the same Being who commands us to love mercy, says also, 'Do justice'; and therefore I have no objection to give the colonists whatever relief may be due them for any real harm they may suffer as a result of losing their slaves."

Wilberforce's proposal seemed little different from motions that he and Buxton had proposed—and that had been rejected by Parliament—every year for years beyond counting.

To anyone looking on from the sidelines, the speech of this frail old man must have seemed a waste of breath. But when a beam of sunlight suddenly burst through the window and lit his face, Wilberforce exclaimed: "Freedom is bright before us. The light of heaven beams on that goal and that light is a promise of success." Somehow, despite all the opponents lined up against him, Wilberforce made it sound as if he believed victory was near!

If he was correct, however, it soon seemed obvious that he would never see the victory.

By early May, a month and a half after he made the speech, he was confined to bed and fighting for his life.

On May 14th, the Colonial Secretary gave Parliament a stack of petitions signed by almost a million and a half Englishmen. The petitions asked for the slaves to be completely freed. Stanley also presented a Bill to Emancipate[2] the Slaves. The Bill said that all slaves should be freed in one year. The freed slaves should then be apprenticed to their former masters for 12 years. Furthermore, Stanley's Bill said, in order to ease the difficulties for the owners who would lose the services of their slaves, the government should guarantee to the slave owners loans worth £15 million.

When Stanley ended his speech, it was obvious that neither the slave-owners nor the Abolitionists were satisfied with his proposal. At the same time, however, neither side seemed ready to object to it … at least not in principle. The planters simply pointed out that loans would be of little value. And the Abolitionists protested that 12-year apprenticeships were far too long.

So Stanley modified his proposal: give the planters an outright *gift* of £20 million, and shorten the apprenticeships to seven years.

On July 24, 1833, the gift of £20 million was approved in committee. It passed by a vote of 158 to 151. The next day, the shorter period of apprenticeship was passed. And the day after that, on July 26th, Commons passed the whole Bill. No one doubted the Bill would pass Lords.

When Wilberforce was informed of the vote, he said,

---

2. *Emancipate:* free.

"Thank God that I should have lived to witness a day in which England is willing to give £20 million to abolish Slavery!"

Having lived to see his life-long dream achieved, it was is if he had been given freedom to die. The next day, a Saturday, his health suddenly worsened. By Sunday, July 28th, he was in a coma, and at 3 in the morning on July 29, 1833, he died.

One year later, almost to the day, at 12 midnight on July 31, 1834, 800,000 slaves were freed in all the British territories.

One of Wilberforce's biographers, Reginald Coupland, wrote, "It was more than a great event in African or in British history. It was one of the greatest events in the history of the world."

Questions

1. What is the meaning of the word *emancipate* or *emancipation*?

2. What were the two key pieces of the British Bill to Emancipate the Slaves?

3. Wilberforce said he had "no objection to give the colonists whatever relief may be due them for any real harm they may suffer as a result of losing their slaves." What does that mean?

CHAPTER 16: WHAT ELSE DID WILBERFORCE ACCOMPLISH?

Besides the Abolition of Slavery, Wilberforce worked vigorously toward the "reformation of manners" in British society. And he made significant progress in this area even while he made noteworthy contributions to other matters as well.

The Proclamation Society

One day Wilberforce observed to a friend that when a society values religious faith, there often seems to be a great deal of religious hypocrisy. People pretend to be more devout, more righteous, than they really are. But, he said, "I wonder if we now have a different kind of hypocrisy? Are people now acting *worse* than they would if left to their own devices? Is it possible that they think it is *fashionable* to be immoral?"

This thought particularly bothered him as he considered how British society responded to class distinctions, the differences between rich and poor.

He realized that—just as we see today—poor people were fascinated by the rich and famous. Moreover—and as is also common today—the wealthy often got away with truly outrageous behavior. A wealthy man who became drunk and killed another person might receive a mild "warning" and be let go. Not so for the poor. A poor father who stole some food to feed his family could be—and, too often, was—hanged for his offense.

Wilberforce reasoned that if the poor follow the example of the rich, then the rich themselves need to act better. Change needs to start at the top. Improved behavior of the wealthy could prevent a major source of grief in poorer households (not to mention in the wealthy households themselves).

As he was thinking about these things, Wilberforce noted that the kings of England traditionally made special Proclamations when they were crowned king. These Proclamations had been a tradition ever since King William and Queen Mary came to power in 1692.

King George's Proclamation of 1760 was typical. It spoke against excessive drinking, blasphemy,[1] profane swearing,[2] and other such things. In his Proclamation, King George also urged his subjects to do good. All persons of honor or authority, he said, should set good examples and seek to help reform "persons of dissolute and debauched lives."[3]

So the king himself seemed concerned about the issues that disturbed Wilberforce.

Wilberforce discovered that when William and Mary issued their Proclamation in 1692, public morals had actually improved. But the Proclamations since that time had made almost no difference at all. People ignored them. He wondered why.

As he studied the issue, Wilberforce noticed that William and Mary established local Societies to help government officials detect crimes. The kings who issued Proclamations after William and Mary never established such Societies. They simply issued Proclamations.

So, Wilberforce thought, did the Societies make the

---

1. *Blasphemy:* insulting or showing contempt for anything sacred.

2. *Profane swearing:* often called bad language, foul language, swearing or cursing. The adjective *profane* differentiates this kind of swearing from thoughtful swearing or oath-taking such as is required in courts of law ("Do you solemnly swear to tell the truth, the whole truth, and nothing but the truth ... ?").

3. *Dissolute* and *debauched* refer to unrestrained immoral behavior: getting involved in gambling, drugs, drinking and so forth ... and caring not one whit about how your behavior affects others.

difference? What if we created such Societies—or one such Society—today?

And so he determined to form a group to promote the idea that it is *fashionable* to do good. "Maybe, then, people who are trying to make names for themselves by looking as bad as possible might change their behavior. Instead of trying to outdo each other in appearing wicked, perhaps they will seek to engage in kinder and more considerate behavior."

As a result, in 1787, just a few months before the Committee for the Abolition of the Slave Trade approached him, Wilberforce founded the Proclamation Society. The Society would call people to pay attention to the king's Proclamation. Its members would do whatever they could to encourage people—especially the wealthy—to conduct themselves with integrity and greater concern for public morality and, in the end, hopefully, influence British society as a whole for the better.

Society for Bettering the Condition of the Poor

Some critics claimed that Wilberforce was only concerned about slaves and showed little interest in British laborers' working conditions. But long before they raised these objections, Wilberforce had helped found the Society for Bettering the Condition of the Poor—a group that worked to establish laws to improve working conditions.

In particular, the Society sought to improve children's working conditions and to restrict their working hours. Wilberforce helped to draft the labor Bills and supported them in Parliament.

In 1802, he helped pass a Bill that ended forced apprenticeships. It forbade the cotton and woolen mills from having apprentices work after 9 o'clock at night, before 6 in the morning, or for more than 12 hours a day. (Yes, prior to that time, children often worked more than twelve hours in a day!)

By 1817—15 years later—you could hardly find any apprentices. Apprenticeships had been almost completely eliminated. But they had been replaced by child "wage slaves." So the Bill that controlled the working conditions for apprentices still had no effect on nine out of ten child laborers.

As a result, the Society pressed to limit the conditions under which children could work. For example, they proposed that children younger than nine should be banned from working in cotton mills or factories. They also sought to prohibit employers from requiring children aged 16 and younger to work more than twelve and a half hours a day.

It took five years (from 1815 to 1819) before Parliament finally agreed to the legislation.

Broader Impact on British Politics

As we have already seen, Wilberforce wanted British culture to become more moral. His goal for society as a whole impacted Parliament. As Garth Lean writes:

> When he began, Wilberforce was one of ... three members of Parliament vaguely identified with "vital Christianity." In the next fifty years, over a hundred Members sat in the House who thought as he did and an equal number were active in the House of Lords. Their presence did much to transform the House from a club mainly concerned with the interests of its Members to an assembly responsible for the public good. He and his friends introduced wider issues and established that these ... issues ought to be decided not by ... self-interest but by moral right.
>
> During the succeeding century, statesmen, to be successful, were compelled to live, or at least pretend to live,

morally and for the public good. This, as Wilberforce had foreseen, increased the amount of hypocrisy shown by some politicians, but more importantly, it established politics as an honorable profession for honest men.[4]

Wilberforce led Members of Parliament to focus on issues of justice rather than personal self-interest. He and his friends also developed new methods to arouse public interest in the business of Parliament ... and, as a result, to *influence* Parliament.[5]

The leaders of the American Revolution had used newspapers, pamphlets, petitions and sermons to shape public opinion. Then, through the public, they changed the opinions and policies of their government leaders.

Britain, however, had no similar pattern of political influence. The methods that Wilberforce and his Abolitionist friends used to influence public opinion: their use of petitions, articles and pamphlets, their appeals to pastors to help shape public opinion: these were all new to the English political system. The Abolitionists' example set a pattern that political leaders have followed not only in Britain, but elsewhere around the world to the present day.

British Colonial Policy and International Relations

In 1793, the charter for the East India Company came up for its 20-year review in Parliament. Wilberforce knew that many of the men involved in the Company believed that British relations with India should be solely of a commercial and political nature. The Company should do nothing to encourage one type or discourage another type of moral or religious views. It had no responsibility

---

4. Garth Lean, *God's Politician* (Colorado Springs, CO: Helmers & Howard, 1987), p. 131.
5. Lean, p. 182.

to educate Indian nationals.

One might think such a view is enlightened. After all, it left the people of India to make their own decisions about how to educate their children and how they wanted to live.

In practice, however, these men's "neutral" attitude spilled over into strong hostility toward anyone else from England—and particularly Christian missionaries—who wanted to go to India and participate in any form of educational enterprise. The East India Company leaders were at least as hostile toward the missionaries as any representatives of the Indian people themselves might have been. And what bothered the Company leaders wasn't merely the missionaries' religious teachings. They opposed the missionaries' efforts to establish quality (non-religious) educational and medical facilities, too.

As you might imagine, Wilberforce determined to change the Company's policies. He moved that the Company charter should permit it to select and send out schoolmasters and chaplains in different parts of India. The motion did not *require* that such people be sent. But it did say that such behavior should be *encouraged*. The Bill was defeated.

Wilberforce and his friends immediately determined to produce a better result when the next 20-year review came around in 1813. In the years that followed, they gathered information about the situation in India. They took careful note of Hindu customs that seemed particularly offensive to most British (who had been raised in a biblically-influenced society). Examples of such practices included *suttee*, in which a man's wife is burned to death (or throws herself on the funeral pyre) when her husband dies; the caste system, in which large segments of the population are treated worse than animals; the practice of human sacrifice; and so forth.

Wilberforce and his allies were convinced that the presence of missionaries in India could change many of these societal evils.

In March of 1813, when the Charter again came up for review, Wilberforce and his friends were ready. And they applied the same tactics they had used in their efforts for Abolition. Besides gathering information, they enlisted the help of pastors, sought to educate the British population about what was happening, and circulated petitions. By June, they were able to present Parliament almost 2,000 petitions that contained the signatures of more than half a million people.

The petitions alerted the Members of Parliament that, even if they didn't personally care about India, or even if they were personally opposed to the idea of Christian missionaries being permitted in India, the MPs had better pay attention to what Wilberforce and his friends wanted to say. The British people were watching.

Over the course of the debate, ten of Wilberforce's closest friends spoke in favor of his proposals. Wilberforce himself spoke for three hours to a packed House. One reporter wrote in amazement: "Much as I differed from Wilberforce in opinion, it was impossible not to be delighted with his eloquence. He never speaks without exciting a wish that he would say more."

"It was an extraordinary performance," writes Garth Lean.

> ... Making the most of the horrors that the debate had revealed, he exclaimed: "The remedy, Sir, is Christianity.

Christianity was declared by its Author as 'Glad tidings to the poor,' and, faithful to her character, Christianity delights to instruct the ignorant, to care for the needy, to comfort the sorrowful, to visit the forsaken."

Wilberforce denied he was advocating compulsory conversion. "Compulsion and Christianity! Why, the very words are incompatible." He was not asking Parliament to organize Evangelism, he said. He was asking for toleration, "that we should not, in effect, prevent others from engaging in it."[6]

From a position of almost certain defeat in March, Wilberforce's proposals not only passed Commons, but Lords as well. And it became a part of British policy around the world for the rest of the 1800s. It changed Britain's treatment of nationals not only in India, but throughout Africa, too.

Lean writes: "This victory meant that the British Parliament had for the first time officially recognized that Britain had responsibilities as well as opportunities in India." And that was a great advance.

Prior to Wilberforce's policy, it had been the general practice of British businessmen and soldiers to completely ignore the concerns and interests of the people whose lands they invaded. As far as they were concerned, their responsibility was simply to enrich themselves and the British Crown however possible. But, writes Lean, the new policy "'marked the change from looting to paternalism.'[7] ... Paternalism is not a popular word today, but it

---

6. Garth Lean, *God's Politician* (Colorado Springs, CO: Helmers & Howard, 1987), pp. 116-117.

7. **Paternalism** comes from the Latin word *pater*, which means father. A person or government that is paternalistic treats others like children. Such a person, for example, might restrict others' behavior "for their own good." Laws that require you to use a seatbelt or to wear a motorcycle helmet are often criticized as being paternalistic. Parents who forbid their children to jump off the roof of their house, or hospitals that refuse to let psychiatric patients have metal utensils in their rooms—utensils that they might use to kill themselves—are also said to be paternalistic.

was a great advance on looting."[8]

Other Matters

— Besides the Proclamation Society, Wilberforce helped found several other organizations for social change, including the Society for the Suppression of Vice, the Church Mission Society, the Society for the Prevention of Cruelty to Animals, the British and Foreign Bible Society, and the Freetown colony in Sierra Leone, Africa.

— He supported Elizabeth Fry and her work in prison reform.[9]

— He believed the British criminal code was cruel. Even as late as 1820, there were over 150 crimes that could be punished by death in Britain. Some examples of such crimes: shoplifting,[10] petty

---

8. Lean, p. 117. One can readily question Lean's rather rosy view. We should note, for example, that, even after Wilberforce's policy was put into practice, and *despite* the policy, looting and abuse often continued. Indeed, one might examine Britain's performance over the next century and a half and say that government policy and practice continued to favor exploitation. Britain was, by and large, as much the domineering and overbearing empire it had ever been. And yet …

If nothing else, the educational systems established by the missionaries throughout the British Empire sowed seeds of self-respect and self-determination on the part of the educated classes in the conquered territories. And those seeds eventually yielded the fruit of colonial independence.

It is also true that, in theory, at least, and as a matter of stated principle, there were grounds for protest on the part of the oppressed and there was a possibility that British officials might be found guilty of abusing their positions within the British bureaucracy.

9. Fry is well worthy of study in her own right. For a quick introduction, you may want to visit this page at the BBC: http://bbc.in/efry01.

10. *Shoplifting* generally means taking merchandise from a store without paying for it … with the intent to use it for one's own benefit. In other words, the shoplifter is clearly doing wrong, but he or she is not stealing as a kind of "business." In Wilberforce's day, many people were so poor, it was not uncommon for children to steal food from bakeries or butchers' shops just to stay alive. But if they were caught, they could be hanged.

theft,[11] or cutting down a tree in a public place.) As a result, he worked to change the laws.

— He was obviously concerned for the poor. Knowing how great the gulf was between rich and poor, Wilberforce favored a tax on incomes. He himself gave away a third or more of his income to worthy causes and to individuals in need.

— He often spoke in favor of causes that others of his class tended to oppose. In the case of the American War for Independence, for instance, he urged Parliament to let the Colonies go. And though the French revolutionaries behaved in horrifying ways that alarmed the English leaders ("What will happen if people here in England adopt similar tactics?"), Wilberforce urged Parliament to remember the injustices that had pushed the rebels to fight in the first place.

Questions

1. What was the Proclamation Society?

2. What do you think of Wilberforce's idea of "a different kind of hypocrisy"? Do you think it is possible for people to think it is *fashionable* to be immoral? Can you think of any examples of people who do things because "everyone" around them acts that way—things they probably wouldn't do if fewer people acted in that particular manner?

3. What was the Society for Bettering the Condition of the Poor? Do you think it was a good thing that Wilberforce helped found the Society for Bettering the Condition of the Poor? Why or why not? Give some examples.

---

11. *Petty theft* is distinguished from grand theft. Petty theft involves stealing a relatively small amount—in today's society, perhaps, something under $500. Grand theft would have to do with stealing a lot more. The point, here: people were hanged for petty thefts—stealing $100 or $10: picking someone's pocket, for example.

4. What changes did Wilberforce bring about in British policy toward countries around the world as a result of his Bills designed to permit Christian missionaries, pastors and teachers in India?

5. What does Lean mean when he says that Wilberforce's policy in India "marked the change from looting to paternalism"?

6. Lean says paternalism was "a great advance on looting." Do you agree or disagree? Why?

7. How did Wilberforce change British politics?

POSTSCRIPT

William Wilberforce was involved in far more matters than those I have been able to discuss in this book. His life, too, included a far greater number of fascinating experiences than what I have been able to convey.

I hope you will be inspired to follow Wilberforce's example in pursuing whatever you find yourself drawn to do in your life.

Question

1. As you think of Wilberforce's life, what most impresses you about him? Is there something he did—a character quality he showed, perhaps—that you would want to emulate? Why?[1]

---

1. There is no "answer key" for this question. I expect you to answer it for yourself.

ANSWER KEY

Chapter 1

1. When and where was Wilberforce born? *1759, Hull, England.*

2. What significant event happened when Wilberforce was nine years old? *His father died.*

3. What did Wilberforce's mother not like about Aunt Hannah and Uncle William Thornton? *They were "religious enthusiasts"—which meant they followed John and Charles Wesley in trying to live their lives according to the demands of the Bible.*

4. The author claims that Wilberforce had very little in his favor to make him a world-changer. Why is that? *Because he was small, not very good looking, had very bad health, was encouraged to waste his time ...*

5. What did it mean to "foin"? *To engage in verbal contests to see who could tell the best joke or make the wittiest comment.*

6. What kinds of things did Wilberforce and his friends like to do? *Sing, dance, drink, gamble, foin, go to parties and banquets.*

7. This chapter begins with a story about how Wilberforce's mother, friends, and even professors at college all encouraged him to play rather than to work hard. In fact, some of his professors actually criticized him for studying: "Why should such a wealthy man like you trouble himself with study?" What do you think? Is there a reason someone—whether wealthy or poor—should study? *This question asks for your opinion. But here's what I think. If Wilberforce had had any idea what he would do later in life, I imagine he might have said something like this: Whether rich or poor, boys and girls, men and women, all should study* in order to prepare themselves to do something great with their lives—*something more than they could do if they fail to study.*

Chapter 2

1. What university did Wilberforce attend? *Cambridge.*

2. What is an MP? *Member of Parliament.*

3. When did the British Parliament tend to do most of its business? *In the afternoon into the evening (or even all night).*

4. What are the names of the two Houses of the British Parliament? *Commons and Lords.* Who served in them in Wilberforce's day? *Commons: people who were elected; Lords: nobles appointed by the King and clergy.*

5. What did Pitt do that no man has done before or since? *He became Prime Minister at the age of 24.*

6. What is the Prime Minister? *He is the man with the most power in British politics (after the King). He is similar to the U.S. Vice President, Speaker of the House, and Senate Majority Leader all rolled into one.*

Chapter 3

1. Describe what life was like for wealthy people in Britain at the time Wilberforce first entered Parliament. *They would spend most of their time eating, drinking, dancing, singing, foining, gambling, and so forth. Life, to them was "a dream in which they could do no wrong."*

2. What was life like for poor people? *"A nightmare in which they could do no right." They—men, women and children—worked 13 to 16 hours a day or more six or seven days a week. It was a grueling existence.*

3. How about for slaves? *It was as bad as for poor people only worse. They had no legal protections at all against harsh or unjust masters ... .*

Chapter 4

1. Why did the relationship between Pitt and Wilberforce change in 1785? *Primarily because Wilberforce had determined to follow what he believed God was telling him to do. That meant he would no longer do what his "party" told him. He would make his decisions on Christian principles. At the same time Wilberforce made his Christian commitment, Pitt was becoming busier in broader government issues ... .*

Chapter 5

1. How did Wilberforce's life change after he became what he called "a real Christian"? *He began to do "Christian" things like say a prayer before every meal and try to turn conversations so he and his companions would talk about spiritual matters. But more than anything, he became quieter, more sober, more thoughtful, considerate and even-tempered.*

Chapter 6

1. What was the Committee for the Abolition of the Slave Trade? *A group of men, mostly Quakers, who wanted to do whatever they could to get Parliament to pass a law that would abolish the Trade.*

2. What kept Wilberforce from presenting his Bill when originally planned? *1) He lacked the information he needed; 2) he was so sick, he almost died.*

Chapter 7

1. Lord Penrhyn said, "It is absurd to suppose that men, whose profit depends on the health and vigor of the African natives, would purposely torment and distress them during their passage so as to endanger their lives." What do you think is a good response to such a statement? *How about these? 1) "We aren't supposing: we have looked and seen with our own eyes what is happening"; 2) "It is absurd for men to do the kinds of things we have observed; so let us make a law to protect fools from their own foolishness and the poor Africans from the fools' cruelty … ."*

2. What did Pitt do in order to get the Lords to pass Dolben's Bill? *He told them that, if the Bill lost, he could no longer sit in the same Government with anyone who voted against it. In other words, he would force a new election… .*

Chapter 8

1. Summarize the arguments both for and against Abolition of the Slave Trade. *For Abolition: the Slave Trade is evil, unjust and unkind. Against Abolition: it's not really necessary to abolish the Trade, the Slaves don't really have it so bad; if you do abolish the Trade, it will ruin many merchants as well as the British economy.*

2. What observation finally determined what the House was going to do with Wilberforce's motion? *The observation that all the evidence against the Slave Trade had been gathered by the Privy Council and not the House.* Why did this matter? *It really didn't. But they pretended it did. They said, "If we do not demand an independent inquiry of our own, then in the future, the Privy Council can say that they have done their own work and we must trust their information."*

Chapter 9

1. After the initial debate (described in the previous chapter), the MPs who spoke in behalf of the Trade stopped arguing so much and instead engaged in other tactics to stop the Abolitionists. What tactics did they use? *First, they tried to slow down the inquiry, then they tried to get the House to make a decision based only on the testimony that had been given in favor of the Trade; finally, they suggested gradual abolition.*

2. Dundas made two major proposals. What were they? *1) That the Trade should be regulated; 2) that the Trade should be abolished "gradually."*

3. Why would Dundas' proposals possibly seem good both to people who were *opposed* to the Slave Trade and to those who were in *favor* of the Trade? *They would seem good to those who were opposed because they sounded as if they restricted the Trade; they would seem good to those in favor of the Trade because, in truth, though they sounded tough, the proposals really did little if anything to alter the Trade's day to day operations.*

Chapter 10

1. Pitt died in January 1806. This was how many years after the Committee to Abolish the Slave Trade had asked Wilberforce to champion their cause? *They had asked Wilberforce to help them in 1787–19 years earlier!*

2. Counting the Bills he presented in 1789 and 1792 (as well as all the ones mentioned in this chapter), how many Bills did Wilberforce present to Parliament in order to limit or Abolish the Trade? *Eleven—including two in 1793.*

3. Why would Pitt's death have been discouraging for Wilberforce? *First, because Wilberforce was losing a great friend; that is always depressing. But also because Pitt had supported him strongly ….*

Chapter 11

1. What did Stephen mean when he said that his proposal would "place Parliament in a position of limiting and not merely regulating the Trade …"? What is the difference between *limiting* and *regulating*? *Limiting meant there would be places where the Trade would not be permitted to operate. Regulations simply place specific restrictions on the manner in which the Trade could operate.*

2. What does it mean to say that something is "a Government issue"? *It is being proposed by the Prime Minister and the Cabinet—the highest members of the government. The matter has greater weight than something that is proposed by those who have been elected to office.*

3. Explain Sir James Mackintosh's statement that "We ought … to marvel that it would take but the short span of one man's life to remedy the miseries of millions for ages." What was he saying? *We tend to think that tasks take a long time when they take more than a few months or years. In reality, if in our lifetime we can achieve some goal of lasting and widespread value (as Wilberforce achieved for the slaves – yea, millions over many, many years), then we have every reason to be thankful.*

Chapter 12

1. Why did the Abolitionists come to the conclusion that it was not enough merely to abolish the Slave Trade, but they had to abolish the entire institution of Slavery? *Because as long as the institution remained, there was too great a temptation to circumvent the laws against the Slave Trade; furthermore, they came more and more to the conclusion that the institution itself was wrong.*

Chapter 13

1. List at least four things Wilberforce did that enabled him to influence other people. *He was pleasant to them: he always tried to avoid hurting them; he asked thoughtful questions and listened carefully to their answers (because he was genuine-*

ly interested in what they had to say); he took care to think of the kinds of questions and concerns that people who would oppose him might have—so that he would be adequately prepared to answer their questions and concerns; he was humble: he didn't try to prove how smart or great he was; he permitted other people to shine while he remained in the background.

2. Wilberforce obviously held strong opinions about religion, slavery, and other topics. But he seemed, generally, not to offend people. How did he avoid offending people? *By being gentle, kind and humble. He wouldn't look down his nose at other people with whom he might disagree. He showed genuine interest in other people by asking thoughtful questions and listening carefully to their answers. He was courteous, pleasant, and cheerful.*

3. No matter how winsome you may be, it is almost impossible not to cause offense to some people (as Wilberforce apparently did to the old nobleman). Why is that? *Because if you stand for something—if you are consistent and steadfast—people will know it. And your very presence will be a reminder of the thing(s) you stand for.*

Chapter 14

1. Describe the Wilberforce family's manner of life. *Rather hectic, disorderly, loud and affectionate! Examples: breakfast, at which 33 people—of all different varieties—might be present; the servants who seemed to "do their own thing" and not worry too much about what Mr. and Mrs. Wilberforce would say (since they almost never said anything in rebuke or direction); the kids and Dad playing games together; Dad not being upset even when he has lost an important paper and the kids are making unbelievable noise … .*

2. What do you like about the way the Wilberforces lived? *Of course, there is no answer key for this question. You need to answer it for yourself.*

3. What do you dislike about their manner of living? (How would you do things differently?) *And there is no answer key for this question, either. We're asking what you think!*

Chapter 15

1. What is the meaning of the word *emancipate* or *emancipation*? *To free; freedom.*

2. What were the two key pieces of the British Bill to Emancipate the Slaves? *1) a £20 million payment to the (former) slaveholders; 2) seven-year apprenticeships for all the (former) slaves.*

3. Wilberforce said he had "no objection to give the colonists whatever relief may be due them for any real harm they may suffer as a result of losing their slaves." What does that mean? *The slaveholders had paid money to purchase their slaves. If the government now freed the slaves, the slaveholders would lose the slaves' labor. They paid for the slaves because they expected to get the value of the slaves'*

labor. Now, if they lost their slaves, they would have paid for something (the slaves' labor) that they would never receive. Therefore, to make up for that loss, Wilberforce was saying, he was willing to pay them for the loss of their slaves, but they would have to prove that they really were going to lose the services of the slaves they claimed were their own.

Chapter 16

1. What was the Proclamation Society? *A group formed to encourage people—especially the upper classes—to pay attention to and honor the King's Proclamation concerning vices. Its purpose was to reduce the temptations for lower class people to fall into behaviors that might lead to the gallows.*

2. What do you think of Wilberforce's idea of "a different kind of hypocrisy"? Do you think it is possible for people to think it is *fashionable* to be immoral? Can you think of any examples of people who do things because "everyone" around them acts that way—things they probably wouldn't do if fewer people acted in that particular manner? *(We want your opinion. You'll have to think this one through on your own!)*

3. What was the Society for Bettering the Condition of the Poor? *A group focused on improving working conditions. They were particularly concerned for working conditions for children.* Do you think it was a good thing that Wilberforce helped found it? *(Your opinion !)* Why or why not? Give some examples. *(Children who were working long hours in dangerous conditions could not go to school ...)*

4. What changes did Wilberforce bring about in British policy toward countries around the world as a result of his Bills designed to permit Christian missionaries and teachers in India? *He helped awaken Britain to its moral and cultural responsibilities. At least* theoretically, *it had no right merely to look out for its own interests and ignore the interests of the people in the lands it had conquered; it had no right merely to engage in commercial trade and pay no attention to the social and moral problems of the societies with which it dealt.*

5. What does Lean mean when he says that Wilberforce's policy in India "marked the change from looting to paternalism"? *Britain's foreign policy before had been primarily concerned with how much it could gain financially from its colonies ("looting"); now it realized it had an obligation to show concern for its colonies, the way a father should show concern for his children ("paternalism").... .*

6. Lean says paternalism was "a great advance on looting." Do you agree or disagree? Why? *(Of course, these are questions for you to answer!)*

7. How did Wilberforce change British politics? *He helped wake up the entire Parliament (which was made up almost exclusively of upper-class people) to their responsibility to show concern for people other than themselves—i.e., especially, to the lower classes. He helped them see that they needed to make decisions on the basis of moral principles rather than personal or class interests. He also helped establish the*

practice of seeking the input and influence of popular opinion on decisions of Parliament.

Postscript

1. As you think of Wilberforce's life, what most impresses you about him? Is there something he did—a character quality he showed, perhaps—that you would want to emulate? Why? *As with other such questions, I expect you to answer these for yourself.*

ANNOTATED BIBLIOGRAPHY

Anstey, Roger. *The Atlantic Slave Trade and British Abolition 1760-1810.* Atlantic Highlands, NJ: Humanities Press, 1975.
> This is a scholarly book written to answer a Marxist attack on Wilberforce. The Marxists suggest that slavery would have died of natural causes with or without Wilberforce. Anstey argues that the Marxist thesis is bunk. Not truly a biography of Wilberforce, yet it touches on matters of serious concern to any open-minded student of Wilberforce and the Abolition of Slavery in England.

Coupland, Reginald. *Wilberforce: A Narrative.* Oxford, England at the Clarendon Press, 1923.
> This is one of the finest biographies I have ever read. Footnoted, a beautifully written narrative, it is full of direct quotes and background information. I had the strong feeling, as I read it, that "I was there." *However,* this book is written by a British professor for an adult audience: his very proper British sentence structure and his vast and sometimes archaic vocabulary (especially when quoting original sources) will make this an unlikely source even for most high school students.

Lean, Garth. *God's Politician.* Colorado Springs, CO: Helmers & Howard, 1987.
> Easier to read than Coupland, this biography is shorter and not so elegant. Lean provides no footnotes. He places greater emphasis than does Coupland on Wilberforce's wide range of interests and his achievements beyond the slave trade.

Pollock, John. *Wilberforce.* New York, NY: St. Martin's Press, 1977.
> Well-researched, more up-to-date than Coupland, a sourcebook for Lean. I used it on occasion in preparing this volume.